The Book  Funnels

The Book of Funnels

Christian Hawkey

Verse Press ~ Amherst, MA

Grateful acknowledgment is made to the editors of the following publications in which many of these poems first appeared: *The American Poetry Review, Conduit, The Colorado Review, Denver Quarterly, Green Mountains Review, Massachusetts Review, NC2, Volt,* and *Western Humanities Review.*

Thanks to my mother, Adrienne Adams, who was the first to bring me to words, & to the friends who helped assemble the poems in this book: Rob, Earl, Dara, Michael, Lisa, Jim, Michelle, Tony, & most of all: Lori & Z. Also thanks to Robert Green of Amherst Typewriters for keeping the machines clean.

Published by Verse Press
www.versepress.org

Library of Congress Cataloging-in-Publication Data

Hawkey, Christian, 1969-
   The book of funnels / Christian Hawkey.– 1st ed.
       p. cm.
   ISBN 0-9723487-9-4
   I. Title.
   PS3608.A89B66 2004
   811'.54–dc22

                              2004002985

Available to the trade through Consortium Book Sales and Distribution, 1045 Westgate Drive, St. Paul, Minnesota 55114.

Cover photo: Untitled, by Panos Kokkinias. Used by permission of the artist.

Book designed and composed by J. Johnson
Text set in Bembo. Display set in Bureau Grotesk.
Printed in the United States of America

9 8 7 6 5 4 3 2 1

First Edition

CONTENTS

THE ISLE OF MONAPIA

A thought drones in, trailing its landing gear—I can't shake it,
this papery nest of wasps lodged above the eaves,
my eyes, which is fine,
let them come,

come and go, some catacombs are only ash, never meant to be dislodged,
some foreheads simply ladders
—a few wrinkles,
a few rungs—

ribs that float a little to the left with each breath,
each step, I love the way our hands
close neatly inside another's.
There is a photograph

of a photograph of you, submerged in a blue aquarium.
There is the way certain faces seem always
to have risen from water,
floating above us,

steaming, streaked with rain—a flash of lightning
and the bolt of landscape unrolled
for our arrival is cut in half;
we jump back

under a purple beech, the last place we want to be.
Look, that rivulet beading off the brim
of your hat is a sign,
all the argument

we need to stay here, safe, the clouds like drawers
opening, one by one, closing off the sky.
Yesterday I pulled off
the road

to watch a vertical sunset—red, fluorescent tube slicing through clouds—
and a man pulled alongside me and pointed,
nodded through the passenger window
and drove on . . .

redundant, I thought, yet oddly reassuring, a category
99% of life falls under—perhaps this is why
we spent our afternoons
under the porch,

studying ankles, tracing footsteps, the difficult speech of chairs,
a thought being passed around, dropped,
an ice cube falling back
into a glass,

evening backing into night—and then the radio, faint, *today two nations
exchanged remains,* or memories, tomorrow a city will disappear,
and the only language I want to learn
is Manx,

from the Isle of Man, or Monapia, which no one recalls, except in sleep,
a dream of snow, light crackle of snow dissolving on an ocean
with no islands in sight . . . a periscope breaks the surface,
looks around, withdraws.

LOVE, CHARCOAL, WEATHER VANE

I left a book out in the rain and the rain won
—no contest—which is why I refuse
to drink water, mostly, some
people enjoy

hanging their life on an adverb—and the book
was, by the way, a dictionary:
neon mold bred through the
word decay, down to

decor, defenestrate, dehisce—the last spores dusting
the word delude and dendrology was perfectly
clear, and though I can never recall
the names

of trees I love them, especially this wispy
one with tiny leaves that shimmer with
a little wind in sunlight
like water

with a little wind in sunlight—a quaking oak? No—and I've never trusted
moving, blinking stars—I've never believed
there is only one pronunciation
in the sound of

our names: for three eternal seconds waiting in the checkout line
I couldn't recall my own: Boris? Hadrian? Larkspur?
Gone. I needed a name tag. I needed two.
My little mound

of groceries moved closer—but does it matter, really,
what we're called? Call me Really. Really Fine.
And a great many of certain pretentious ones
we will call Particularly

since they're discussing, each time they use the word,
themselves. I'd like to go by X. Sometimes I do:
If $x + y = z$, and we let y stand for
you, not You

but the you whom I turn and address, suspiciously
(myself), then z will be the third I long to be
fired in the purity of equations
—and what are numbers

but wishful thinking? I've yet to stub my toe on a
natural number, or any number other than
love, charcoal, weather vane
which is why

my only response to my credit rating is laughter—hysterical—
why herons, blue, embody
so much grace
they leave me

disembodied, speechless, holding my breath, holding my breath
—there it goes—and why sincerity is a way of gazing
that makes another's gaze
turn away,

why I can, sometimes, taste complex minerals on your tongue,
why people we've met once, in passing, show up
in the lower right-hand corners
of our dreams

for the rest of our lives—patterns occur, recur, occur, recur, etc.—
which is why any creature, when chased, cuts
unpredictable angles through the landscape
and why, additionally,

why, finally, the innumerable stars on a cold, rinsed night
make me feel at home, even though I'm lying,
lying in the middle of a razed corn field
freezing my ass off.

NIGHT WITHOUT THIEVES

The day is going to come—it will come—put on your nightgown,
put on your fur. And yea unto those who go unclothed,
unshod, without fear, fingering the corners
of bright countertops

and calmly, absentmindedly, toeing the edges of clouds
drifting in a puddle. Put on your deep-sea gear,
your flippers, and walk to the end
of the driveway.

It will come. Be not afraid to chase large animals.
Once, I had a conversation with the eye
of a moose, looming wetly
through the branches.

I was terrified. I froze. I backed away. I imagined it.
And then on the other hand there are those
truly fearless: schools of silver minnows
darting in and out

of the gills of blue whales—how many invisible organisms
do we sustain without knowing it? Our own,
for one. Put on your crowded body,
like Vallejo,

who pulled the sea over his shoulders in the morning
and stepped firmly onto ground. Thus,
when the day came, he conducted
electricity

perfectly—unknowingly—and wrote by the red light of his teeth
after a glass of dark wine. Put on your lamp shade.
Put on your cage. If, in the shape of a key,
the shape of a woman,

a bank of swollen clouds surging over the tree line,
a word basipetally descends
break it open: how *pome*
and *granate*

meet in dense honeycombs, red seeds erupting inside a mouth.
And though we lose eleven eyelashes a day
by blinking alone we cannot enter
the Kingdom,

nor can we move sideways, high on this narrow goat path,
without the proper footgear; a pebble's kicked loose,
and the echo returning
from the ravine

sounds like an avalanche, and is. Put on your helmet.
Take off your clothes. If anyone even *thinks*
about laughing
it will be

the end of us—Rita, hand over the kazoo. Thank you.
Now hand over the other one. Good.
And in case of an emergency
realize, quickly,

there is no emergency and move on. Like a thief in the night
the day came. Then night came,
and emptied out its thieves
into the furious sunlight.

BECAUSE WE ARE STARVED OUR ENTRAILS SPARK

A hawk barks in the mews. Dawn begins.
Our leather hoods—loosening, loosening.

A warren of cottontails
quivers underground. Tunnels

are their nostrils. & upwind a breeze
assembled by what it

passes through: steam
withdrawing into

peat bogs, an old dog stretching
—the grunt of it—water beads

tightening the underside of a leaf.
I have visited this scene before.

I was put together here. I will spend a life
making wind chimes (the wind will be my partner).

I will spend another with a goat
(pupils of soft rectangles, floating

on a pond of gold). I will fall asleep
with doorknobs, a different one each night,

& I will reserve the glass ones for old age
that I may dream with perfect clarity.

Hunger is the first emotion. Also the second.
Some part of my face is always in shadow.

Some moles navigate tunnels with a pink star

for a nose. They shrivel when exposed to light.

She waited by the window while I undressed
in the dark. I wanted to touch

what the forest had left
behind the leather hoods

of her eyes—only the feathers, she keened impatiently,
only the feathers. Wind chimes shook the air.

A mole breathed. My entrails sparked.
She swiveled her head toward the sound.

She swiveled her head & her body followed.
Entrails the color of electrical cords,

I almost said flowers. Entrails,
white cotton, a rip along a seam.

The look of wonder, pulling it out.
One cloud. Then two.

A COPPERY RAIN SLASHES THROUGH IT

How behind the fly mask
the eyes of a horse
overflow? And how the lather
rising from its flesh?
How the white shrouds
rising from the lake?
How when you look away
does a cloud divide in two?
How mitosis, how divorce,
crows afloat on a patch of snow?
How the black wicks, waiting to be lit?
How the moss, with its love of mist?
How the stones, covered in moss,
the earth, covered in stones,
sky under the cover of stars
sliding over the hood of a car?
And the mobs, the strange bombs
dropping through the night
with women painted on their chests,
the cloud cover, the nimbostratus,
the laughter echoing in a darkened
stairway, the song, the whisper,
the half-whispered password of a stream
swollen underground with rain
—and then the greeting, and then the kiss

UP HERE IN THE RAFTERS EVERYTHING IS CLEAR

Night, night was a quick-thrash from the gator-pond,
the silence, just after, widened out in rings,
even the fire ants in the dry grass
held still. Hold still
said the branch, lifting in the absence
of an owl, hold still. A blacksnake
measured distance with a flick
of its tongue.
And as the Keeper of a Crooked Nose you could tell us
the wind contained three corridors:
Spring Rain, Goat Over the Hill,
Something Died in There;
as the Student of the Horseshoe Crab
how to use a gathering wave
to work deeper
into sand.
Later, you learned to laugh like that, knowing
it was a better way to close your eyes.
Only in the Subkingdom
of an Empty Cistern
did you allow hands to be upholstered
by an underground stream;
there are no words
for this sound.
Once, perhaps, you knew them, before buildings
unfolded from the ground at your approach,
before the rain descended
in a column of newsprint,
smudging the pane, and others arrived,
leaving dents behind—P.
with his photographs
of skylights,
afraid to leave his apartment, or M. complaining
of too many rivers in her poems.

The Allegheny, the Arno,
what is a map
without blue veins? Strange the way we pound ourselves out again
and brighter for it, usually. Left with a gaze
that seemed to arrive from such a distance
as to watch itself
you listened, the way a cat listens, to a wall (knowing the wall is listening back).
What did you hear? A few phrases, quick feet, an eardrum
suddenly fluttering, like a moth's wing,
of its own accord,
as if it were someone else's and not your own.

SINCE JUDGMENT IS ALSO A STORM

Everywhere there's water: heavy rain spun into wind-sheets
shakes out across the newly turned potato field;
two, three cows hunkered down into stones.
Are you there?

Listen, the oak loses a leaf by the minute,
each with a rust-bruise, speckled,
like a moth's wing, one camouflage
burning inside another

at the edge of one's body: obsidian blown
in the hourglass of a wrist—your bones
were never dry enough for me.
Have a seat.

What did we listen for? One clear icon after another
straying through an
open window.
Close it,

let requiem fall from someone else's hands;
yours passed through me and returned
to your chest—I knew then
we cannot

observe the way a childhood erases a person,
how, during the night, a landscape can
accumulate: I woke to a thin wall
of snow

along the curve of your body and held my breath.
A wind rattled the sill. I watched a crow
gun across the ceiling and then I
crossed over to you.

See how it takes its time, follows, like anything else, the river.
If we are the surfaces that have run through us
then the hollow click
of my heels

through the peach-marble atrium, the simple elevator ding,
doors revolving into mango groves, sweet pulse
of the rose apple tree is one
I cannot forget,

or high over the Gulf of Mexico the infant tornadoes
reaching out of the clouds, fingers of a slate hand
feeling for something dropped
down the grate of this world,

golden—yes, to pull the eye—and retrieved by a child
years from now with a piece of string, pink gum,
humming a song we have yet to hear,
softly, like thunder.

But soon it will arrive, bend the willows into a deeper prayer
—from where I stand, back flush
against the house,
I hear you

enter the room for the last time, shut the door behind you
like a locket, pause at the blue aquarium light
and think the poised fish in their
"sepulcher of rain"

have never moved, white flags unfurled above the cobalt
gravel, speechless as the first three stars of evening.
Fine. Even the perfectly sheltered
take shelter

at the approach of a storm. There are things we can't measure. Play it safe.
Even the wind seems to argue that everything matters.
What's left? Wet bark, dark architecture
against a moving prop of clouds.

THE BOOK OF FUNNELS

Unhoused casements

         snap of tongues on a teeth-ridge, alveolus of the. Or,
out of boredom searching my face in the mirror I found a vein,
and searching the vein I found a scar, smooth as slate,
and searching the scar I found a name, an old name—there were serifs—
the name of a city I'd forgotten, which I whispered,
I don't know why, I was alone,
and the Whispered City unfolded a map of streets I once traveled
         wet cobblestones, *contradas,*
         a horse led through the doors of a chapel

To the pleasure of hundreds

         a sacred, steaming manure

Fräulein, can you

              sometimes, when I can't sleep, I drag my sleeping bag
into the meadow's precise center
& crawl inside, head first. Fräulein, there is the stars'
ceaseless drilling. I close my eyes. Somewhere below me
a star-nosed mole cuts its webbed hand
on a shard of glass. I close my ears .
& over my body the current of a young doe
eddies, ripples across the field, a low-lying midnight fog
swirling after her, falling back, suspended. I know you are close.
The scar across my cheek burns. I think of reentering
           your atmosphere,
           your long, burning hair

Don't move. The slightest motion

           & this landscape, erased by floodlights

One cold cloud

                    at the edge of an obscene green.
And a few cows, kneeling around a tire.
I drag my tether to the pond. I place my hand inside
and it tilts up, like a cheval glass, creaking,
the sky slides quickly away. I turn,
looking for my glasses, I don't need them,
a jay saws the air—in half—in quarters—
this corner of the field where I am staked down
to the cold shadow of a
                    blue cloud,
                    folding over my own

Somewhere in the trees

                    I hear a toilet flush

There is a Queen inside

                      she cannot speak—with a yellow sponge I wet her lips
but only slightly, I am terrified
of her voice, of her enormous, rolling body
& the groans that move through it as if through rooms—when someone knocks
I simulate her voice *gravity is a dwarf factory, how light a caterpillar steps*
by her soft, trembling stomach I know she is laughing
& withdraw, closing door after door after door
until I can barely hear her, rain
outside an open window, a cigarette quietly glowing, *I am an arctic flower*
my Queen I can barely hear you, I am standing on my toes
                    at eye level
                    an electrical socket

Two faces,

                    one above the other

Dust

              duodenum, umbilical rain, fist; temple, sextant, skeleton key,
ant; whispercourse,
eleven holes, over the counter, life;
box of tissues, box of tongues *leather shoulders in the rain-soaked fields;*
adamant, unfailing, parrot throat, ice; whereof inorganic tears, digital saliva,
chamber of pixels, chamber of clouds *rain floods the edges of an intelligence machine;*
next please, thank you, omnivorousness, bleach;
password, blue word, bullet hole,
smoke; strap-on emotions, updraft of equations, visible ribcages
transparent chests. . . . It was the ant
               that she wanted,
               such love as a colony

& a mind above ground, balancing

              the weight of a leaf by the measured distance from its hole

A shyness, tilting

                the black, opal eye of a mourning dove
widening, absorbing morning,
& a figure approaching, a figure on all fours,
morning on all fours, absorbing a windowsill, flakes of yellow paint,
a figure crouched there, a bird crouched there,
a figure wrapped in the sphere of its eye, a window on all fours,
crouched between them, wrapped in fear, a bird listening,
a figure listening, night puts one foot down, the glass exhales,
another foot, the bird exhales, tilts its black, convex eye
away from the figure
                vigilant
                on all fours

Dawn. A stream of hot urine

                parts the hair on my left thigh

Come to think of it

Don't. Don't even. Either a landscape supple & pliant or,
either a seagull nowhere near the sea, either a saint,
Franciscan, the miniature feet of sparrows
crimping a human finger (delicate article
—pause—paradisaical, O . . .
O what? What do the weak, milky eyes of angels
know of gravity? Or the way one's sense grounds
to one side
when an ear
fades out
—cavernous
thought
with a zero breeze
            lashed
            to the back of it—

It's a goat's breath, thistle clean

        light fog on the monitor's screen

A blue chair

                            awaits our arrival. As though we were shadows
at night moving slowly toward each other
through the white room of a blizzard. Wait.
There's something in your eye.
At a given distance it's hard to discern whether two figures
move together or apart; a given instance
in which the smoky web of a spider
holds together our legs. Slumped
in a blue snow bank, fumbling with a blue-tipped match
I negotiate
                    a stream of particles
                    without end, except here

A face across from me,

                    the red warmth of soft breathing

& then the miniature sheep

                   sighed, turning their nervous eyes
from the sleeting wind, & then the sleeting wind
formed ice-helmets around their fist-sized, fluffy heads,
& then their heads were heavy, & hung low on their small shoulders,
& then their helmets fused with the snow gathering over the field . . . .
& when they sighed for the last time their breath filled
the helmets, & turned to snow, & the snow worked its way
inside the pink chambers of their tiny ears
until it leaked, slowly, onto their miniature, shivering brains.
Then they were truly deaf, & truly blind,
                   unable to see
                   the one arriving

On enormous snow shoes

          wielding a tire iron

What horses

                             rising from the violin bow
how many voices, frayed,
gallop through my ear? One, but his fetlocks
are knotted with burrs, and when he lowers the pulleys of his neck
his eyes stay open at the trough.
In the absence of wind
it is the same trough the sky inhabits.
My face leans in
and slides over the red Coke can, lolling at the bottom,
until its bullet hole opens out of my eye. Heartache.
Which is the other horse,
                    beautifully groomed,
                    standing beside me

Ready, with each whinny,

                    to take a bite out of my shoulder

Your face

                    an ember, orange, hitting water, extinguished.
I heard it. Heard while the words were hurled,
no, before hurled—picked out the hottest coals.
All the paintings in the room hung crookedly.
I removed my wig and laid it on the table.
I removed my glasses and placed them on the wig.
I removed my lips and tucked them, gently,
under the glasses. You didn't laugh. Together
we breathed a long time alone while the face,
between us, watched a ladybug
                    push a dead fly
                    off the windowsill

One more hour, thought the face,

            one more hour

GOYA'S GROTESQUERIE

I don't know the story of his last days
but they ended, as always, in walls,

& what are "they" but so many palms
lining the dictator's long drive—

he's in the Yellow Room
smoothing his glass moustache,

he's sipping Lapsang souchong
& feeding a piece of cuttlebone

to a caged nightingale—tired bird.

★ ★ ★ ★ ★

But the wall on which we rest a hand
swivels us into the room

behind it: here's an X-ray
of a woman with her back turned:

she holds a wooden pail of water
in one hand, an umbrella in the other

—was it raining in the room
when he painted over it,

the pastoral scene not yet dried?
Not yet. How do you give yourself

a second chance? Take away the first
with a brush drawing pigment over sand

& lime & water—pushing the figure to motion,
a god dancing with a child in his mouth.

& what led historians to the scene
with their ghost machines of particles,

of "penetrating various thicknesses of all solids,"
of "producing secondary radiations

by impinging on material bodies"?
Given the walls, & the metal plates,

given the substitute for light
what did you find—the shadow

of a woman in between, lost, Queen
of the Kingdom of Thin Fossils . . .

★ ★ ★ ★ ★

—to believe in the grotesque, the griseous,
fever-stained fur of a raccoon

that burned, like a hot stone,
a hole in the snow before it died,

one paw curled, the other relaxed.
"Relax. There's more here than meets . . ."

But how do you meet the eye?
With a red parasol? A pail of water

brought to the blind donkey
waiting in the oblong shade of a barn?

Or two versions of the same woman:
one clothed, one naked, one man popping

his child in his mouth—one surface
in the room that was raining when Goya

woke, walked downstairs in the dark & began
while the woman, over whom he painted, laughed

(in the Yellow Room with all the windows
the nightingale, beneath a canopy of blankets

steps down, pauses, removes its jeweled hood
& sets out to explore the bottom of its cage).

THE NERVOUS MAN IN A FOUR-DOLLAR ROOM

Inside a stomach full of butterflies & flies
a thought churns, flutters, rises,
& I cough up a monarch stickily into spring.
Tender gastronomical flower. Milkweed sneeze.

& always, on my right side, the world waits,
on my left side, honking. A car drives off.
I've missed my ride. Behind the curtain
behind the window behind the screen the sky

sifts pollen, shifts clouds, trades stars
for one star—sunlight, sunlight, there you are.
Light never gets bored with the world.
Confession: I do—with light, never the world, thus I

wear a blindfold, loosely, some things are better
glimpsed, in passing: a coccyx, a childhood, an axe.
& by the seat of my guts I move forward,
straight into a wall—hello wall—by the seat

of my lips I speak sideways, into an ear,
any ear, my own, which never fully formed,
is deformed, is simply a hole
in the side of my head where a car horn

passes, where a light rain swirls,
where light reigns & little else.
All sounds find a hole & disappear.
What remains? A stomach, churning. A man

in a room in a corner in a chair wearing a blindfold,
which he removes, folds, slides into a bag
& stores, in a drawer, & leaves, in a rush,
hitting the light switch, slamming doors.

WHATEVER IT TAKES

Then on the fifth day with the absence of crows
came ice. In the slow accumulation of hours
the crab apple sagged,
a glittering ice-spider guarding the lawn.
I shielded my eyes, turned sideways,
slipped inside.
A small wind, the size of a leaf, scuttled around us.
I say "us" because I wasn't alone,
there was a voice
like a prayer, the sound of green wood
creaking under weight.
This is stupid,
I thought, but the tree was old and ready to break
so I swung my arms through the icicles
—they snapped crisply
like bones, bird bones, transparent remains of animal
crystallized by centuries
but it was only ice,
hours of it, and I was sweating from the work
moving from limb to limb
shards fell around my eyes
if my hands were bleeding I didn't notice.
A truck drove up and I froze.
He set the package
on the ground, passed the clipboard through the branches.
I signed and offered him an apple.
Which he took, and stepped back
without saying a word.

NOTE LEFT BEHIND ON A TABLE

A window out of a kind of absence
translates the night, offers my face
and beyond it, a thick memory,
a few constellations, loose change.
On the other side of this paper
is a portrait of you. I drew it quickly,
too quickly, and when I came to your mouth
I held my breath. My body rocked,
and I got it all wrong. Perhaps
as you read this your lips
are half-open. Perhaps it is night.
And when you look up, a face
in the window, yours, but not all yours.

I RETURN TO THE O's IN OBLIVION

I return to the O's in oblivion
as a tongue returns to a beautiful wound,
a wound returns to the clarity

of a scar—smooth as cellophane—
touch this, says the child, touch here
and the story begins, turning on an I,

esophageal forest, wind in the trees,
laryngitic whispers as if we were useless
and we are, says the landscape, we are.

Scowling he withdrew beneath the grape arbor.
Wasps sucked champagne from bursting globes
and stumbled into the air, mechanically.

His aorta pulsed. His mind pulsed back.
Along the horizon a garden hose snaked.
Black clouds rushed in, taking their places.

Somewhere a child smacked into a wall
and fell back, too stunned to cry
—freeze it—too stunned to cry

at the turn of a wrist
a world opens, and turns over—a yellow wasp
coated in foam, dropping backwards

into the past, watching its future recede.
Adrienne, the rain never arrived.
I left your sundress on the line

for weeks, wind filling its empty sleeves.
Nights I took it down and put it on,
gently, in the backyard, large man

in a white dress, soaking up the moon.
Nights I took down, gently, and put on.
White moon soaking in the backyard.

THISTLES FOR FINCHES

He was supplanted, gradually, with thoughts
lifted from the red lips of a sleeping infant,
the mass note of starlings, yanked into silence,
from a sonogram of shadows, flitting over his chest,

—white cells, red cells, an illuminated text.
A thermometer was inserted. Inserted and removed.
Every thirty seconds ovulation occurred.
Every thirty seconds a lifetime occurred.

Digitally altered. Digitally removed. His eye
clicked on a heron—he didn't need his hands—
his eye clicked on—his eye clicked on
and it wasn't enough, he needed his fingers,

he needed his nails, though they were pocked
with white craters, undernourished by the clouds.
He sat in black soil, digging with his hands,
he came across a bottle sealed by the past,

starlings resumed in the sycamore tree, joy-
seeds bursting from their narrow beaks
(the recording crew retreated, grating their teeth),
he opened the bottle and a blue odor escaped,

the word *grace* bubbled up and issued
from his lips: he wanted to howl, with his tiny chest,
heave a clear rain into the landscape.
He wanted to laugh like a red trash can

kicked down a flight of stairs
but he did nothing—nothing at all—
all that had never occurred to him before: leaf-fall,
the wherewithal, blink if you understand this.

HE SPOKE AND, SPEAKING, REALIZED HE COULD SPEAK

He rose and, rising, left his head behind him
on the pillow. He turned and, turning,
asked his head to join him but the head refused,
rolled to one side and began to dream,
twitching, began to weep, openly,
to laugh, ebulliently,
shout orders, grovel, gasp, whistle casually
until the body began to miss the head.
He left and, leaving, asked his body to follow
but it refused—his knees shook, his chest heaved,
his testicles withdrew, swiftly,
so he lay back down, joined the head
and waited. Rapidly the sun revolved,
filling the curtains, darkening the room.
A fever. A cold sweat. A cold compress.
This was the great battle: memories
clashed, switched sides, changed clothes
and clashed again; emotions were used,
used up and discarded. The head was in heaven,
overactive, in control, but it wasn't,
the body was, or so it thought,
which the head allowed. Rapidly the sun revolved,
darkening the curtains, emptying out the room.

SPRING FEVER

Something tapped my retina. It was the sun.
It wanted my attention. I had none.
I was busy thinking about myself, nursing myself,
which was easy, since my breasts were swollen.
Everything was perfect. I thought I was alone.
I wasn't. The sun was there, like a new religion.
And my neighbors were out with it, swinging
yellow chain saws between their legs.
A man eased himself under a car: another religion.
On all sides: fanatics. Inside: fear.
That one will arrive, knock on my door,
ask me what I believe in. What do you believe in?
I can't believe I just asked this question.
Amazing. I believe in that. And my cat,
who doesn't believe in me (it makes it easy).
And a small wind, filling out my throat.
And a second wind, which arrived late,
with a sneeze, and begged my forgiveness.
And a third wind in the shape of a lion,
padding across the roof. And a fourth wind
from the east, carrying the ocean on its back.
And a fifth wind swirling at my feet, helplessly.
And a sixth wind with bloodshot eyes,
dragging little bits of embers, little bits of ash.
And a seventh wind. And the seventh wind
is the wind that never arrives: stillness.
I believe in stillness, how we move through it
with our eyes closed, our mouths open,
breathing in the eighth wind: blue triangles, red squares.

SLOW WALTZ THROUGH INFLATABLE LANDSCAPE

At the time of his seeing a hole opened—a pocket opened—
and left a space. A string of numbers plummeted
through it. They were cold numbers.
They were pearls.

And though they were cold the light they cast was warm,
and though they were pearls he thought they were eyes.
They blinked. He blinked back.
Anything that blinks

must be friendly, he thought, until he saw the code
—a string of numbers—carved into their sides
and grew afraid. He tried to close
the space

but it was no longer his own. He tried to close his eyes
by they were no longer his. He tried to close
his mouth, his hands, his ears
but they were no longer

his, were never his to begin with: this was the time of his seeing.
The world opened. A line began. A tree grew above him
and he thanked it. A sun dawned over the line
and he thanked it.

A building unfolded abruptly and blocked the sun
and he put his hand on its side and thanked it
for the shade, he put his hand
on the sidewalk

and gave thanks to the cement—it was cool and wet and
took the shape of his hand into it—he put his eyes
at the feet of a woman
and she lifted them,

to her own, and he thanked her, from the inside, and she understood.
Wires swirled above him, straightened out along an avenue
and the lights came on. One moon rose.
A second moon

rose on the windshield of a car and he thanked them both.
This was the time of his seeing. This was the time.
An electric green beetle shuttled out
of the darkness

and landed on his forearm, pulsing, he didn't remove it.
It seemed relieved. Some things work very hard
to leave the ground. Somewhere an infant
called out, sharply,

was comforted into silence. The deep note of an owl opened a tunnel
in the air. He was growing tired. He didn't want to stop.
The world opened.
A line began.

It traveled out ahead of him and returned, tracing a wave,
white foam gathering, gathering the moonlight,
black water rising into a wall
and he held up his hand:

the wall froze, trembling, the head of a seal
poked through, looked around, withdrew,
he liked the way its whiskers
bent forward

as it withdrew and he liked the way his hand had stopped a wave
so he thanked his hand and moved on,
into the outskirts, the taste
of salt on his tongue,

the taste of brine, it made him thirsty although he had no thirst.
This was the time of his seeing. This was the time.
And the skeletal shadow of a radio tower
loomed to the right of him,

creaking, a red gleam, then nothing, he thought he heard music
passing through him and he was right:
he was humming something
from a song,

but he couldn't remember the words, which was fine,
they were sentimental anyway so he
thanked the radio tower
and kept moving,

the road turning to gravel, the gravel turning to dust,
the ditches sang with frogs, the ditches were silent,
a pair of yellow eyes waited for him
to pass and so he passed,

calmly, since the beetle was with him, trying to refold its wings,
and the tree was with him, unfolding its leaves,
and a man was with him, walking at his side
—he didn't need to ask

who he was, so he didn't, but in the corner of his eye
he caught a glimpse: he seemed familiar,
he looked like him
and he was,

although a string of numbers was carved into his side.
He asked if he could touch them and he said Yes,
touch them. They were cold numbers.
They were pearls.

He asked if he could kiss him and he said Yes, kiss me, and so he did.
It was a strange kiss. It was a beautiful kiss.
It seemed to last a long time.
It seemed to last a lifetime.

GREEN SOLITUDE

No such thing as exit for the man lost
In the middle of a cornfield.
No such thing as field.

A disinterested wind wanders up,
Unravels the silk
And moves on.

It's late summer. The ears have burst.
He passes and suddenly the stalks
Are discussing his absence,

A conversation that follows him, barely overheard,
That makes him stop
And turn around.

John Clare wrote of a green solitude
After the hustling world was broken
Off; no one followed

On his way home through the fields.
He laid his head down to the north
To show himself

The steering point of the morning.
When he woke, it was winter,
The stalks

Cut down and covered in snow.
There were no dreams.
Only a voice

That he knew was near, not his own,
And he listened, for a minute,
To the cold wind

Before finding the road again, and the sound
Of his listening was the landscape
Advancing at his approach.

THE ART OF NAVIGATING IN THE AIR

Quickly, quickly, we have a few seconds left:
with centipedal lips
I kissed a dark shoulder, passing on my left,
the day has five heads, which one is your own,

one foot alive, in the video-stream, red flares
up ahead, along the side of the road
—how the drivers swivel their heads
impassively, like dolls—and this is where I carved

your name into a fallen log and fled,
into the underbrush, when the log groaned.
The day has five heads, which one is your own,
I woke on the banks of the Connecticut,

it could have been the Tigris: a herd of goats
upwind, observing from a bluff,
a rustle of silk along the trail, Sardanapalus
has come to bathe—you have a beautiful name,

I said, it sounds like loneliness, and I waited for him
to hit me but he didn't, he kissed my shoulder,
he gave me his robe, the day has five heads,
we have a few seconds left, which one is your own:

a second, split, a clump of bloody feathers
frozen in the air—reverse it—and a bird emerges,
whole, from the turbine, and flies off
like a graceful thought at 30,000 feet

above sea level, which never varies, although
our eye level is constantly changing:
I fall to the ground, to see what I can find,
someone's been here before me: they've labeled

all the stones, tagged each blade of grass
(I've been here before me, moving among the weeds).
I blow on a dragonfly, it refuses to move,
it glints like a microchip, I think I'm being recorded:

a sliding glass door, sliding shut, muffled
laughter behind the pane—O that the light
of the incubator is still warm, and soft,
O that I will make it beyond the backyard . . .

Once he kicked a red ball over the fence.
Once it was over it was in his mind.
Once it was in his mind it began to grow.
He thought it would stop. It kept growing.

Red food. Red walls. Red trees. Red water.
Red eyes. Red mind. In the mirror,
however, his face was blue and he was thrilled.

SEARCH PARTY

Can't see it but I hear it—helicopter blades
chopping through fog, the *whump, whump*
of a thing suctioned, pulled under, gone.
Now they'll search for the search party.

I walk along the interstate, in full view,
cars swerve around me, crying out,
I try not to take it personally.

And a yellow wave, curled on one side
like a lip—lifts—the snowplow
suspends, for a second, its white arc.

Joan, the letter I sent was intercepted.
Have you taken off your clothes?
Have you let your hair grow?

Another is on the way. Wait for dawn
—a flutter of wings—the warbled
underwater coo of pigeon #750499.

HOSANNAS FOR THE TATTERDEMALIONS

I was just standing there when it
reached out and bit me. My taste buds
went deaf—you saw it—you saw it happen—
I was just standing there. I thought it

wanted me to describe the way you smell
the rain eighteen point five seconds
before it falls, softly, before it stings,
sideways, before it ceases, instantly,

as if it had never arrived, which it hadn't.
I didn't hear a thing. We were in the middle
of a psalm and I didn't hear a thing, although
the air quivered, held up by a hundred palms,

although the woman in front of me collapsed
into me, completely, and I saw through her eyes
the pain in her back, pressing outward,
they were my eyes, pressing back, they lifted her

up into the song and the song continued,
the smell of rain on my hands, where it hadn't been.
I was just standing there. I didn't feel a thing.
There on the banks of the Ganges, watching a body

set on a raft, set on fire and set adrift;
there on the corner of East Main and Plum Tree
when the sky darkened, the air thickened,
and a beautiful black fruit slid over the sun;

there in a series of asterisks, annotating
a text (the text was above me, a handful of stars);
there where a memory surfaced, changed
by the surface; where a tongue, caught on a word;

where a cry, caught in the throat;
there in the throat where a breath turns,
turns over, turns into a sound
pulling the ocean into the land, right up

to the mountains, where the cold rivers begin.
I was just standing there, off to one side,
another side of me broke off—a continental drift—
it happened so slowly I didn't feel a thing,

a series of islands, annotating the sea
(the sea was beneath me, a clean white sheet),
a *jangadeiro* unfurls his water-soaked sail
and leans back, over the waves, into the wind,

moving out of the harbor, into larger harbors,
larger sounds, past the Indefatigable Islands,
inhabited by the Indefatigable Ones.

THIRD LUNG

Like a supple idea my tail breaks into segments
at will, and grows back, at will,
and I leave myself behind myself
in the Old World, wonderfully young again.

Just so a glass lizard beneath a heel
laughs into two and moves on, into one
—if cut I bleed greenly, if perforated
I leak openly, like a colander, the mind a red

lettuce head, rinsed and shaken clean.
But it's not clean. It's spackled with the gray matter
of other people's brains, which are larger
than my own—frontally—and breed at a faster pace.

Thus can one stand in the shower
for hours, hot water surging around the chin . . .
And if I didn't want all things altogether
at once this poem, which began with joy,

wouldn't have veered off—segments of a toy
train set plunging over the edge of a table.
Switch it back. *What back?* This back,
the thought-lever. *But I thought it there!*

Exactly—each autumn I detect a drop
in the oxygen level, and I retrieve from deep storage
my third lung, which resembles a smashed bagpipe,
and strap it three times around my chest.

Later, at night, I take it off and place it
next to me, on the bed, where it breathes
calmly and, sometimes, purrs. It produces
more air than either of us could possibly use.

SECRET MINISTRY

I'll whisper this, so I don't wake you,
these are my instructions—I have none—
a red chair dusted with snow,
a throat with a few lesions,

the long binary code of winter
unscrolls, at night, the cat sits
on the sill, memorizing, memorizing,
no use—white grains, black grains,

the video you left for me was blank.
But I watched it anyway, mesmerized,
until a back-draft in the chimney
filled the room with ash, filled it with snow.

INTERLUDE WITH GYPSIES AND TAMBOURINES

Wait a minute. We're not finished with you.
We were discussing the Indefatigable Ones
at a time of Maximum Perforation and Wonders,
the bodies of crows plummeting earthward,

stiffly, thudding onto your porch and you,
you were wearing your Silence Helmet as if it
were a crown, as if it were a kind of prayer.
You can't pay attention to this world on your knees.

And desire isn't a tin can taken into the woods
and shot at; it's a tin can shot to hell
and swallowed, piece by piece, while a crow
laughs—bouncing through the limbs—insanely.

You were checked for explosive residue.
You spread your legs. You emptied your days
into a white plastic bucket. You removed your belt.
You removed your shoes. You removed your heart,

a fistful of shrapnel. You were asked to step aside,
you were asked to step outside, onto the tarmac,
onto a plane—you were being deported,
although no ships were within sight,

and the others that were with you began
to hold hands, began to stammer a song, *whoso*
list to hunt, in the bee-loud glade,
drowned out by turbines, shifting metal flaps,

along a string of lights the plane taxied,
it made a right and kept moving, it made a right
and kept moving, it made another right
and kept moving—we never left the ground.

We were growing old. We started families.
We call ourselves a nation. We have many children.
This is our flag. It will fit in your pocket.
Thank you for the coffee. Can we go now?

A CLEARING

No one spoke, though none of us knew where we were going.
We had left just after dark, the cones of our flashlights
catching the heels of those ahead of us,
steam from coffee cups

rising over our shoulders, warming the faces of those behind us.
One star, then two, floated up like flakes of cork
in a glass of dark wine and followed us
through the trees overhead.

No one spoke, and though none of us knew where we were going
there was a path, narrow, like a deer trail, we traveled,
crossing over empty freeways, dirt roads,
foundations of abandoned houses,

the charred remains of old campfires. We passed beneath
electrical lines, through strips of forest pulled up
like carpet. The air hummed. Our hair bristled.
When the woods thickened

we held branches for each other, secrets passed from hand
to hand. I saw the red lantern of a cigarette
out ahead of me, swinging in an arc;
it disappeared, swung back again.

I didn't notice the birds fall silent. I turned my light on the woods:
the smashed windshield of an old truck
grinned back at me,
and beyond,

a web of limbs, swirling inward, dense, spun by light
—the way it shapes what's already there,
gives it form, or deforms:
the pattern set

in bold relief an amputation of what's behind it—
until the lights dimmed, went dead,
and it was dark along the trail
but we kept moving.

My ears listened for boots catching on stones. My eyes adjusted,
like someone returning to a theater, to the shadows
in front of me—and those passing
in the opposite direction

to the left of me; I hadn't noticed we were not alone. What is it like?
I wanted to ask, but didn't, for I knew they would not
have answered, or if they had, in a tongue
I couldn't understand.

Perhaps they would have answered. Perhaps they said it was like sex
without friction, like a wind in which nothing moved,
a word repeated until it becomes
your name.

I don't know, and by that time I had forgotten why I was there,
or where my hands were, or how my feet were moving,
my eyes seeing without light—and then
we were in a clearing,

a dark tarpaulin overhead, nailed up by stars, the Big Dipper
hung like a mobile on the grid of constellations.
There was the sound of a river, far off,
a wind cutting

its own path through the forest, and something creaking,
the groan of wood but not trees, a dark structure
at the center of the field, a shadow blotting out
half the sky,

propped up by thin poles, ladders, cranes swiveling their long crutches,
the sharp crack of hammers beginning to echo as we filed
past a man who handed out tools—
I was given a lathe.

What do I do? I asked, but he had no face to speak with
so I followed the others, the grass pale and wet,
like anything kept from light, wet because
there were currents

running in and out of the field. They were running through us.
I don't know where they entered, where they led,
but they were dragging the field
along with them.

A voice on the loudspeaker warbled, as if under water.
People shouted orders. The wind was closer now.
A rope had been strung to guide us.
I kept my head low.

CHRISTIAN HAWKEY lives in Ft. Greene, Brooklyn.